Special Thoughts

By

Jennifer Goldberg

This book is a work of fiction. Places, events, and situations in this story are purely fictional. Any resemblance to actual persons, living or dead, is coincidental.

© 2002 by Jennifer Goldberg. All rights reserved.

No part of this book may be reproduced, restored in a retrieval system, or transmitted by means, electronic, mechanical, photocopying, recording, or otherwise, without written consent from the author.

ISBN: 1-4033-3112-X

This book is printed on acid free paper.

1stBooks - rev. 06/11/02

Book dedication:

I dedicate this book to my uncle Jake who was always an inspiration to me, and the teachers at Claremont Ave. School, especially Ms. Burke for the poetry club in third grade.

Table of Contents

Missing you 1
A World of Darkness 4
Spending Life in Fear 6
Another Challenge in Life 8
Clouds 10
Disabilities 11
Dreams 13
Family 15
Life 16
I'll never be the same 18
Father 19
My Feelings 21
Why do they look at me differently? 23
My teacher 25
Remembering 28
Silence 30
Someone Special 31
The Lonely Road 33
The Things that went wrong 35
The First Snowfall of the Season 37
The Greatest Thing in This Entire World 38
Can't Stop 39
The Tragedy 41
When you Died 42
The Problems of Life 43
The World Trade Centers 45
Valerie my closest friend 46
As life goes on 48
Birds 50
Brothers 52
Wondering for that Special thing 53
The Three Special Holidays 54
Fall 56
All I want is a friend 58
Jake 59

Respect	61
Angels on Earth	63
The City Lights	64
The Last Day	66
The Ocean	68
The Soul	70
The Sunset of Spring	72
When I looked at you	73
The World In A Child's eyes	74
Why?	77
The Loss of Dusk	79
The Stars	81
The Unfortunate	83
A Childs mind	85
Please forgive me	87

Special Thoughts

Missing you

I feel so confused I don't know where to go

I'm sitting out here in the lonely cold

Crying and crying more each second

And all I can do is wonder why

I sit here and cry

Over and over again

I never felt this way before

It feels so new

And yet I feel like

This is my entire fault

All these feelings gather up inside

And then they explode

And I start to cry

I can't take this any longer

Look at me I'm a wreck

Because all I want is you by my side

Just to say

Jennifer Goldberg

Its going to all be ok

Because I know you won't lie to me

No matter what the problem is

But now your not here

And I have to do this alone

I take a step

I start to cry

But I keep on going

Because I know

That I have to get over this

Or life will be a disaster

For the rest of the time that I'm alive

So I make it to the end

And what a surprise

I made the right decision

Without you by my side

But even though

I didn't need you my love will remain

In both my heart and yours

Special Thoughts

Because your heart will always lead you through

When you don't know where to go

And as far as I know

You will always lead my heart

And I'll always lead yours

Jennifer Goldberg

A World of Darkness

I live in a world of darkness,

I open my eyes but see nothing but black.

I can hear, touch, feel, taste, and smell,

but I cannot see,

I live in a world of darkness.

Having to imagine everything,

I never could see the outside world.

I never could see the colors,

or a book with pictures.

I must use different things, and senses

And go to special places.

I feel different.

My world is left black,

no red, yellow, orange, or blue

just black everywhere.

I never know exactly where I am,

or what my surroundings look like.

Special Thoughts

I never saw the birds flying,

or a lake shinning in the sunlight.

I never could see anything but black,

in the world that I must live.

Jennifer Goldberg

<u>Spending Life in Fear</u>

I woke up this morning,

and looked in the mirror.

I saw wrinkles on my face,

then I had realized

that I had grown older.

The years past by so quick

What happened to the little girl?

Well she lived a life fear,

a life in the corner,

away from all humanity.

She lived a life of fright,

never to experience anything new.

Now she's older,

and missed out on so much.

All her stories end out

the same way over and over again.

Because everyday of her life

Special Thoughts

She lived in terror.

Now she's sorry

that she was afraid

to do all the things

that her friends always asked.

She sorry she never rode a roller coaster,

or tried to ride a skateboard.

Most all, she's sorry she never faced her fears,

because now she must live a life

always being afraid.

She can face some fears now,

but other things she will never be able to do

because she was to afraid

when she was young.

Jennifer Goldberg

<u>Another Challenge in Life</u>

I see you everyday at this very moment.

Spending time and talking with you

but pretty soon you will be gone.

I can't tell you how much

I am going to miss you.

I've been with you forever.

We've seen people and faced our problems together.

I never lived a day,

without you nearby.

I feel like my heart is crying,

I don't know what I'll do

without you here.

This is harder for me

than you would think.

it would be.

I guess this is just

another challenge in life

Special Thoughts

that I must face,

but sadly this time

ALONE

I'll get through this somehow,

but it's going to take many years.

Jennifer Goldberg

<u>Clouds</u>

Everyday I walk outside and just stare at the sky.

I see all different clouds,

and when I just look at them;

it makes me wonder why there really here,

I wonder if they are messages from the people we love,

but sadly past away

or I wonder if there just water vapor.

I may never discover the answers to my questions,

but I will never stop coming up with reasons.

I will never stop wondering

because it came out to be

my life long dream;

to discover why the clouds are really here.

So even if its five minutes of my time,

I will sit there and just study them,

until I find out the truth,

behind the clouds.

Special Thoughts

<u>Disabilities</u>

In the past years that I've been alive,

I've heard people saying, "oh look at them",

just because they're different.

I can only imagine how they must feel,

when people point and stare,

as they pass by.

There face may have scars around it,

or they may be missing a limb,

but is that such a reason,

to judge them so quickly.

Are looks more important?

Than a kind loving soul.

Why did the world change?

Where have the hearts

of the people disappeared too.

Don't they have respect?

Don't they understand how these people must feel?

Jennifer Goldberg

I only wish that everyone,

would just talk to them,

instead of automatically assuming

that they can't do this or they can't do that,

just because they're a little different.

How do you feel when someone calls you names?

Just think about it,

That's how they feel,

when they walk outside.

So just look into your heart,

and make them feel,

that they are no different,

than you and me.

Special Thoughts

DREAMS

Dreams always seem that they're fake.

But really there showing your strongest wishes

and the things you desire.

Sometimes they're make-believe,

but usually

they're the things,

which are going through your mind.

Whether it involves you or your friends and family,

or maybe it's something

that shocked you

and maybe destroyed your heart.

But whatever they are,

you should always watch carefully,

Because maybe

One day in the future,

Something will happen

and you'll remember

Jennifer Goldberg

        your dream.

    It may lead you through

       in the safest way.

  So never doubt your dreams,

And remember their not just make-believe.

Special Thoughts

Family

When I look outside

I see a lot of things.

I see the wind gliding through the sky,

and the mountains standing still.

I see the clouds drifting high up in the sky,

but then I see something in the corner of my eye,

It's remarkable,

its like a miracle come true.

It's the thing that makes the candles burn,

and flowers bloom.

Most of all it fills my heart and soul,

It makes my eyes fill up with tears of happiness.

All my life I've been looking for them,

the ones who help me solve my problems,

and escape my greatest fears.

Now I found them,

My family.

Jennifer Goldberg

Life

Life is full of decisions

that we must face and get past.

Life is full of problems

that may hold us back,

until we face our fears

and find out how strong we really are.

Life may seem unfair at times,

but life allows us to move forward;

towards our dreams.

Life gives us existence,

and experiences to grow from,

that helps us form

into a better person.

Into a greater more understanding mom,

or a fantastic, enjoyable, loving dad.

Life gives us sparkling oceans,

green trees,

Special Thoughts

and flowers of every color.

Life gives us things to do,

and puzzles to get past,

life is unbelievable,

in every possible way.

So never doubt life,

and be happy with what you receive.

Jennifer Goldberg

I'll never be the same

Just yesterday you were standing next to me,

now you're far, far away.

I'm sitting on the ground,

its dark outside,

and the stars are shinning bright.

All I see is your face,

high above the city

and all I can do is wish you were still here,

instead of laying in your grave.

Every night I cry and cry until I fall asleep,

I dream of the place where you and me

will never separate,

oh how much I wish this dream was true.

You meant the world to me,

and you still do

Even though you are far upon me now,

so as long as I live, I'll never be the same.

Because I'll always be thinking of and loving you.

Special Thoughts

Father

When I close my eyes,

I see everything that happened in my past.

I realized that every time,

it would always be you and me.

In a way,

you've always lead me through

the hard times.

We can handle anything,

and we will always be by each other's side,

no matter what.

We will cry together,

and never alone.

We will always make sure

that everything is okay,

no matter the day.

So I want you to know,

you will never be alone.

Jennifer Goldberg

I will always be there,

by your side,

so we can face any problem together.

Special Thoughts

My feelings

Every night I look up in the sky

and I wish the same thing over and over again.

I wish this war were over,

and all of us went on with the lives we originally had.

I wish that we would never fight again,

because I'm afraid.

I'm afraid of what might happen to me, and all of my friends

and the people I don't even know.

I'm afraid even though,

I have the strongest trust within my country.

My feelings are just repeating over and over again,

and they're all the same.

They are all saying, Oh my god why, did this happen and why

is there a war?".

I don't know the answer nobody really does.

It's sad, but we must remember that it is ok to be afraid.

You shouldn't have to push away your feelings,

Jennifer Goldberg

because you want to honor your country.

You can still honor the country and be afraid,

because no one in this world is not afraid.

Everyone is at least a little afraid.

Special Thoughts

<u>Why do they look at me differently?</u>

Everyday when I walk around.

People always stare,

and look at me differently,

as if they don't want to go by me.

Nothing really has changed,

I just got a little older.

Twenty years ago,

people looked at me in

the regular way.

They never ran away from me.

What changed?

Why does everyone see me this way?

I just have wrinkles on my skin,

and my hair has changed to gray.

Why can't people see?

That I really haven't changed.

I still have the personality,

Jennifer Goldberg

that I did years ago.

What has happened to this world?

Did looks take over the heart?

Why can't people understand?

I actually never changed.

Why don't they show respect for me?

The way they did twenty years ago.

the only thing left to say,

is that I'll always be the same,

in both my heart and soul.

The only thing that changed,

is the outside,

of my body.

Special Thoughts

My teacher

Christmas is almost here.

There is joy in the air.

Everyone is singing Christmas carols,

and buying gifts.

The children are writing letters to Santa Claus,

And all the families are showing their love for each other.

No one should be alone on these special holidays,

because even if you have been naughty this year you should

still be loved or cared for,

This year I have one Christmas wish,

and it's the one I want the most out of all the times I've been

alive.

It involves someone special that I know.

She teaches me everything I need to know,

and makes sure that I'm ok,

Every single day that she sees me.

She is my teacher.

Jennifer Goldberg

My one Christmas wish is for her one special wish this year to

come true,

because I think she deserves everything in the world,

She gets kids ready to face the world,

every year.

To you she's just another teacher,

but to me she's an elder

that I look up to.

I know that she is a great person,

Just by being with her everyday.

When I'm stuck on math problem she helps me and puts other

things aside,

She is one of the greatest teachers,

and I will always be proud to know that she was my teacher.

She accomplished many things,

and she is a very nice person.

I can tell,

because I traveled many places and saw many people,

and I never saw anyone like her.

Special Thoughts

She's special in her own way,

and understands what happens in our young lives,

So may my wish come true and may her holiday be out of this world.

Jennifer Goldberg

Remembering

I look at you and remember the first time we met.

Then I remember you only have a few years left.

I remember

all the times we had together.

Side by side,

you and me.

I thought we would be together forever,

but now its time to stop lying to myself,

I realize you won't be here for long,

I wished you would be.

Not until now, did I understand,

how much love I carry in my heart for you.

You may not be human,

you may not walk on two legs.

You may be different

than me,

but that doesn't matter to me.

Special Thoughts

I finally realized,

that even though were different,

I still love you more than ever.

All I can do now

is spend all my time with you,

hoping that you somehow won't go.

Jennifer Goldberg

Silence

Every day I see the birds passing by,

but never hear a chirp or a peaceful song from them.

I haven't been able to hear

for along time now.

Sometimes I'm thankful in a way,

but other times I feel like I want to cry.

I wish I could hear just one more lullaby,

one more song.

Oh how I long,

to just hear one chirp,

from a bird.

Oh how a long to hear once more,

It would make me feel complete,

in both my body and soul.

I may never escape the silence,

but I will always be able

to see the smiles on everyone's faces.

Special Thoughts

Someone Special

There are millions of people in this world.

I have read poems, stories and saw movies.

I've heard about a lot of different grandmas.

They say they are caring.

They say they're supportive,

but they don't know what they're talking about.

Until they see you,

your talented in a way I can't explain.

Your love for me fills my body

with strength and dignity.

I've never seen someone like you,

and I never could even imagine

such a person.

You do so much for other people,

but never for yourself.

You put things aside

to hear my problems,

Jennifer Goldberg

with an open mind.

A lot of people say things,

like you're the grandma I never had.

Happily I will never have to say

something like that

because no one in this world could compare to my grandma.

Thank you for showing me

life isn't so bad.

Maybe someday

I'll grow up,

to be like you.

Special Thoughts

The Lonely Road

I'm walking along a road

and all I hear

is the sound of the quiet breeze.

The trees are calm.

There's no one in sight.

I'm all alone

on this very road.

I feel kind of scared,

but yet I feel lonelier.

I wonder where my family went,

and why I'm all alone.

I can't concentrate

because everything is on my mind.

I wonder if I'll ever be in my warm home again.

All of a sudden,

I hear a voice.

It calls for me

Jennifer Goldberg

and everything stops,

and I feel so relieved.

I can barely see the face,

it's blurry because I'm so far away,

I run toward it,

It feels like this path will never end,

then I stop,

and I start to cry.

Suddenly I know where to go

and I make it back to my family.

I learned

that if you trust yourself,

you'll always be ok.

Special Thoughts

The things that went wrong

I stand upon a cliff,

looking at the view,

My eyes won't dare to move,

because of the things I see.

The bright blue sky,

the crystal ocean,

and the trees side by side.

The grass is a forest green,

and the variety of colors in each flower I see.

Then the shinning sun tops if off to give it a wonderful shine,

but then a flash of black came.

When I opened my eyes,

I started to cry

because everything was ruined.

The ocean was polluted along with the air.

There was not a tree in sight,

and the grass was yellow with garbage all around it.

Jennifer Goldberg

This is the world that we created,

but it's not to late to fix it.

If you just clean a little and stop polluting,

the world will go back to that pretty view.

Special Thoughts

The First Snowfall of the Season

When the smell is fresh

and all is quiet.

The snowfall will come

bringing joy,

and love to everyone's home.

The kids will be jumping up and down,

and the adults will be just staring at the view.

Everyone will be doing something,

because it's the first snowfall of the season.

They've been waiting for it day and night,

waiting for the smell of that beautiful snow.

Now its here,

and all they can do

is sit there and enjoy it;

until it fades away,

and spring comes along.

Jennifer Goldberg

The Greatest Thing in This Entire World

Everybody has a different opinion

on what the greatest thing in the world is.

It would be fun to think that its games and toys,

but I think its all the moms and dads in this world.

This might sound a little crazy,

because they make you wear a helmet when you going bike

riding;

and I know they might be a little low on style,

to teens and kids.

When I look outside,

I see them as mature people, who take care of us,

Some people might say

I'm a mamas or papas kid,

but I'm not

I'm just a kid who likes to think that all moms and dads

are the best things in this world.

Special Thoughts

Can't Stop

Our thoughts and sadness,

keep flowing through our bodies.

Over and over again,

we can't stop crying,

because of what just happened.

We keep wondering if our families are okay.

We can't stop thinking,

no matter how much we try

to get it out of our minds,

but it doesn't work.

The feelings we have for someone

will always remain,

in a special part of the heart and will never change.

Because no matter what,

you will never stop loving,

the ones you communicated with,

or even never met.

Jennifer Goldberg

You will always feel bad for them,

and find that you loved them,

more than you thought.

Even knowing the things they might have done.

So don't try to get rid of these feelings,

just think of the good times you had with them.

You must not forget that

our loved ones will always be near,

In our hearts.

Special Thoughts

THE TRAGEDY Sept.11, 2001

The sadness fills the air

Everyone knows soon the bombs will be shooting everywhere

We must hold the flag up high

And not let a tear fall from our eye

We must take all the pain that rushes through our veins

Because of the sadness and deaths that came

We must hold our flag high

And show the patriots that we are inside

And we must not give up

No matter how hard it is

We must protect the U.S. nation

And destroy our enemies' location

If we work as a team

And we do our extreme

We will win, but I know even if we win

The feelings we have we'll stay

But I know Americas strong

And we can handle anything

Jennifer Goldberg

When you Died

When you died

I couldn't sleep

I felt like the sparkle in my heart had disappeared

I thought I let you down

My heart was broken in two

And at that moment

I thought my life was over

It was a terrible thought

Then I realized

A piece of my heart was still there

I lived with it for a while

Until my heart was three quarters full

I knew the one piece that was missing was you

But the memories I have

Will one day fill my heart

Even though you're far away from me now

Special Thoughts

The Problems of Life

There are problems in life,

that we have to face alone.

These problems won't be easy,

they will take a lot of thought.

These won't take a minute long,

they may take even a year.

These problems are different,

than everything else.

Because it's a problem that will,

make you feel

like you don't want to live.

It might make you choose,

between your best friends,

or even a family member.

These problems are a part of life,

that makes it so hard

to survive.

Jennifer Goldberg

It's a problem that will last forever,

even after it ends.

Don't be afraid

Of these problems,

because then the problem

Will be even harder to face.

Always remember you will live on ___.

Special Thoughts

The world trade centers

Towers, planes they don't mix

But just a few days ago they did

It makes me feel so sad I just want to cry

I can't handle this no longer

Because it's eaten me up inside

I have so many questions

But yet no answers

I wish this had never happened

It's on my mind more than anything

It's making me lose control over my life

I can't concentrate

And I can't think

All I can do is express my feelings

This feels so new

But I'll survive

And so will you

Jennifer Goldberg

Valerie my closest friend

My friend's name is Valerie

She means the world to me

She's always there when you need advice

Or when you're just bored

She's always there if something happens

And you need a shoulder to cry on

And hers is always fine

She's always encouraging you to keep on trying

Because her love is set

On the people she cares about

More than she does about herself

She would do anything to make her loved ones happy,

Sometimes she might make mistakes

But you can't blame her for that

Because everyone makes mistakes

She's so important to me

It would be a tragedy

Special Thoughts

If anything happened to her

She's like another mom

When I can't talk to mine

She'll never get mad

But might say a few things to me

Or my family

Only for my safety and her concern

So as you can see

Valerie is more than a friend

She's more than a person

She's my closest friend

Jennifer Goldberg

As life goes on

When we are born

We are like seeds planted in the ground.

Our mothers and fathers water us

until we grow into a child.

We have to learn how to survive,

just like a plant learns to produce.

We keep on growing until we reach a stage.

That's when we grow into an adult and learn how to survive,

just like when a plant learns how to make food.

Are our parents like the sun?

That we can't grow without them.

They help us in every stage of life,

because they went through it before.

We learn that as the years pass,

that we change,

just like a flower blooming in the spring.

When we open our eyes to see the world,

Special Thoughts

It is as if we are blooming,

like the flowers of spring.

We must study how we change,

so that we can learn the cycles of life.

This will allow us to be

mothers and fathers some day.

Jennifer Goldberg

Birds

I wake up in the morning

And look up in the sky

And I see the birds passing by

And its makes me wonder

What do their songs really mean?

Are they from the heart?

Are there music stars for them?

And when they fly together

Are they warning us from danger?

Do they fly away each winter?

For a different reason then snow

How do they see?

Do we look like dolls?

Can birds communicate with

Other birds

Why do they live on trees?

How did they learn to get their food?

Special Thoughts

Are there bird heroes?

Is there world like ours

Maybe some day I'll answer my questions

But for now

It shall lay a mystery

Jennifer Goldberg

<u>Brothers</u>

The wind is blowing past me,

The sun is shinning bright.

This reminds me of the first day,

that I held you,

my baby brother.

With your glistening blue eyes,

Your dirty blonde hair,

And your silky smooth skin.

The minute I saw you,

the love in your teary eyes,

rushed through my veins,

looking for a spot in my heart.

It found one right away,

because I cleared room for you.

To this day,

I can still just look in your eyes,

and know that your love,

will never leave my heart.

Special Thoughts

Wondering for that special thing

For the last couple of days

I've been wondering for that special thing

But nothing do I find?

So I lie down and think, and come up with nothing

So I lie there with a frown

Hoping for just one blink in my eye

And boom I have an idea

But no I can't lie, not once, not twice did this happen

So I lie there and start to cry

I think while the tears are rushing from my eye

Then something happened

I blinked and boom I had an idea

I found it, I pined it, and it was my family!

Now I happily have my special thing

And my tears have disappeared

Jennifer Goldberg

The three special holidays

There are three holidays that I know of

And on these days

You're supposed to show your love

For all your friends and family

You don't have to give presents and money

To do so

All you have to do

Is hug them

And maybe say

I love you or happy holidays

To show them that whenever they need someone

You will always be there for them

And if you live far, far away

All you have to do

Is call them on the phone

And wish them the best day ever

On these holidays

Special Thoughts

It's the perfect time

To get reunited

With the ones that you drifted away from

So may you never be alone on

Hanukah

Christmas

And Kwanzaa

Jennifer Goldberg

<u>Fall</u>

The leaves have change

It's chilly outside

And all I can do

Is stand

And stare at the view

A mixture

Of red, orange, yellow, and brown

Some have three colors

Others only have two

But when you look up in the sky

And you see all the leaves

You can't take your eyes off of them

Until winter is here

Fall is a great time

Just to relax

And enjoy the chilly breeze

Because pretty soon it's over and the trees are bare

Special Thoughts

And the pretty view is gone

But every year

The leaves on the trees

Will be colorful again

But not the same

As any other time

So every time that fall appears

Watch it carefully

Because pretty soon it will disappear

Until the following year

Jennifer Goldberg

All I want is a friend

All my life I've been alone.

Sitting on the bus,

with no one to talk to.

So when I look up at the stars,

I make my one wish,

for me to find a friend.

A friend to listen,

to my problems and fears.

A friend to believe my stories,

A friend to give me advice,

someone around my age,

who I can trust.

Someone who will keep my secrets,

unless they harm me in some way.

All I want is a friend,

That I can call my own.

Special Thoughts

<u>Jake</u>

When I was born

I saw someone beside my dad

His eyes had that sparkle

And his face was nice and soft

He was loving and caring

Along with funny and cheerful

I knew I could trust him

No matter the situation

He used to take me places

About every Saturday

But that doesn't matter to me

Because all I cared about

Was spending time with him

He was like the wings of my plane

Without him I would crash

But then around 1998 November 14

It happened I crashed

Jennifer Goldberg

                He past away

                But I survived the crash

                And made it through

                And happily

                My wings almost grew back

                From all my memories

                So may I say, live happily Jake

                And I will never forget you

Special Thoughts

Respect

As I walk the sidewalks

Of cities and towns.

I start to realize,

that people don't understand.

That people may come from different countries.

They may be of different color

and share different religions,

but they are all human beings.

They deserve to be treated,

just like you and me.

Why do people judge someone just because of their looks?

Why don't they understand,

that nothing can change the personality.

Whether it's your skin,

or your religion.

No one understands,

how your statements may make others feel.

Jennifer Goldberg

You have to show respect,

to rebuild this world.

Otherwise we will never be able

to live together in harmony.

If we show respect for others,

and come together as a family.

The world will solve their problems together.

You will be able to trust everyone.

There wouldn't be anymore stealing,

wars would stop,

and everyone would live in peace.

There would still be problems for us to face,

but we will never have to face them alone.

Show respect.

If you wish to live in peace.

Special Thoughts

Angels on Earth

It is Christmas day.

Everyone is laughing at jokes and spending time

with their families.

A lot of kids think of Christmas as one thing,

and that is presents.

But the only present I long for,

is to have you by me,

on this special holiday.

Your arms seem like wings of holy light.

Every time I look into your twinkling eyes,

I feel love warming my body,

making me feel protected and safe.

There are many people on earth,

but you're different from all of them,

You're an angel on earth.

Jennifer Goldberg

The city lights

As I drive along the road

I look out the window

To see city lights

They shine in different colors

And in different ways

It looks as if the solar system

Is standing in front of me

To me it looks like a valley of shinning stars

But maybe to others it looks

Like just plain old lights

Perhaps the lights

Are representing the stars

Shinning bright down upon us

Instead of up high in the sky

The lights make many designs

And other things in the sky

Maybe it's showing

Special Thoughts

Things that may have happened

Or maybe things you desire

So do me a favor

And brighten your neighborhood

By shinning your house light

Jennifer Goldberg

The last day

Today is a day

I haven't been looking forward to

It doesn't bring me happiness

But yet the opposite

It brings me sadness

I know today is the last time

I'll be seeing you for a while

It hurts me inside

And I rather not show it

On the outside

I tried and tried

To stop you

But it's just no use

You have to do

What life directs you to do

I'll always be with you

No matter if you're here

Special Thoughts

Or miles and miles away

I'll never forget you

You're a big part of my life

And I want you to know

I'll always be there

You write me in a letter

Or remember inside

Because when there comes a time

Even you need my help

I'll always reply your call

With a helpful suggestion

So even though

This could be the last day I see you

It will never be the last day

That I love you

Jennifer Goldberg

The ocean

I sit on the beach's surface

with a few other peers

They laugh and play

but I sit near the ocean

and stare at the beautiful view

The waves build up in an elegant glide

then crash down before my eyes

The shells are picked up and taken away

Soon they will be replaced with another

perhaps from faraway

Far beyond, where I sit

I see dolphins jumping freely

I soon start to realize

that this wonderful ocean I stare at

Is not only a paradise for people

but a home for those

who are marine creatures

Special Thoughts

So now when I see the ocean

that lies before me

Instead of thinking of it as an ocean

I will think of it as a home.

Jennifer Goldberg

The soul

You may think you're a nothing

People may put you down

But never forget

There will always be a person

Who will never say you're a failure

And that person doesn't

Judge you from your mistakes

But from the real person you are inside

You may not always show

The person you really are

But I know that you're caring

Because I can see it in your eyes

Some people think

That you can only show love

By taking them to a fancy restaurant

Or buying them expensive items

But I don't believe in that

Special Thoughts

Because the one thing

That you could give

Is a special part of your heart?

To hold all their love

So never believe someone

Just because their cool

The only thing that can judge you

Is your soul...

Jennifer Goldberg

The Sunset of Spring

The trees have buds all over them.

The sun is down low

and the sky is a light blue.

Then I look in the distance,

and it looks as if it's purple.

The tree branches are still bare,

but the picture isn't ruined.

All winter I've seen the tree branches lonely,

but now spring is here

and the branches have a friend.

The leaves haven't grown yet,

but the view is still so beautiful.

It is the sunset of spring.

It's something I'll never forget,

no matter what is on my mind.

So, as I stand here looking out the window,

watching every moment of the sunset,

I enjoy some of the best hours of my life.

Special Thoughts

When I looked at you

Since the day that I laid eyes on you

I've never been the same

You changed me in a way that I could not

You showed the meaning of life

And you taught me to never give up

You taught me something that touched my heart

And that is that I will never be alone

Because you will always be there for me

If someone else can't make it

And that we will solve are problems together

I never had a friend like you

So caring, loving, and sweet

I will never forget the things you did

And the caring person you are

And I will always be beside you

Because you will always be inside my heart

Jennifer Goldberg

The world in a child's eyes

The world in child's eyes is a puzzle of life with every new step you take. A piece to the puzzle is added every New Year with accomplishments. Finally when the puzzle is done our lives begin to change. We suddenly know what to do, the purpose of life and whom we are inside. We know no matter what, the person inside of us should never change.

Every New Year is a new adventure; every new step is a step closer to the big time. Every new puzzle piece is a new experience waiting to come, and everything new that you experience is a step closer to knowing the true you. The one who knows, that we are more than a kid, worth a fortune and we are more than just cute little girls and boys.

In a child's eyes everything seems scary because we never experienced it before, every game we wonder if its safe and we hope we made the right decision. We hope we stay with

Special Thoughts

the right friends and hope that we don't hurt anyone by doing the things we do because actually the truth is we don't know exactly what were doing because we have so many questions of our own, because we see the world with child's eyes.

Every New Year is a new adventure, every new step is a step closer to the big time and every new puzzle piece is a new experience waiting to come, and everything new that you experience is a step closer to knowing the true you the one who knows that we are more than just a kid and worth a fortune. We are more than just cute little girls and boys.

In adult eyes everything is different, because you know where everything is and the safest ways to go. As kids we don't know, so the world is an adventure, to find the mature persons we are, to find out the answers to our questions that we long to know and hopefully find. We aren't just kids, we are the kids who might save the world or change

Jennifer Goldberg

everyone or even make the worlds biggest discoveries one day. So in our eyes is a new adventure that one day we will hopefully pass and succeed in our greatest dreams_____.

By

Jennifer Goldberg

Age 10

Colonia, N.J.

Special Thoughts

<u>Why?</u>

Why do we fight?

Turn against each other.

We are all people,

citizens of the world.

Why don't we come together?

Save the world, and all its creatures.

Why don't we all become friends?

Live in peace, and help each other.

so everyone has a person to stand next to.

Why do we harm?

Shoot guns, bombs, and missiles,

destroying another's life,

killing creatures that are innocent,

making them a victim.

Why can't we respect all others?

We all live in the universe,

we were all formed the same way.

Jennifer Goldberg

Why don't we compromise?

Save the world its people, creatures, and heavens.

Why is this a mystery?

Something I do not know

a thing that lay unknown

Special Thoughts

The loss of dusk

I sit on the grass

Across from the dock

The sun is reflecting on the ocean below

Giving it a beautiful color

The sky is filled with purple and red

As the boats leave the shore

People are waving goodbye

Others are shouting farewell

Some people are moving away

Others are just going on vacation

So as the people leave

I see a tear strike

From this little boys eye

He shouts will loud

"Goodbye I'll miss you,

please don't forget me

I'll keep you nearby in my heart"

Jennifer Goldberg

The hours passed by,

and the boy was still there looking in the water.

He said, "I wish you were here,

I feel like empty without you"

So I run across the bay

Then I look at him and say

"Don't be sad ".

He'll always be near in your heart.

Life will go on and don't worry you'll be fine.

Just go on as you would and it will feel as if he was next to you.

This is just another phase you must face in life.

Special Thoughts

The stars

I sit outside on a clear night

The stars are shinning bright

And it makes me wonder

Are the stars really made of matter?

Or are they wishes made from people everyday

Waiting to be fulfilled by whoever created this world

And is there shape a special key

To the secret of life, the answer to all our problems

Maybe the stars are actually guiding us through life

Maybe the creator of earth made it for us to follow

So that every person who looked up at the sky

Would know which to go

Maybe the stars are just matter

Or maybe something more

They could be the souls of heroes from long long ago

Or maybe there miracles waiting to be released

No one knows the answer

Jennifer Goldberg

But that doesn't mean we have to believe its matter

You believe what you think stars are made from

And who knows maybe one day we'll discover the truth

Special Thoughts

The unfortunate

Why do they look at me when they pass?

Do I look funny asking for money?

Am I so much different because I live on the street?

Why do they stop talking when they pass?

Am I a different person because I'm less fortunate?

Why do they treat me this way?

What have I done to deserve it?

I can deal with the pressure of surviving each day,

but I can't even breathe when they treat me differently.

My clothes are just a bit dirtier,

and I live on less food.

Is that a reason,

to turn around and run from me.

I could understand,

if I tried to harm you,

but that I am not trying to do.

So don't stare at me,

Jennifer Goldberg

because of my clothes.

Don't make me feel bad,

look at me as you would,

a person sitting on the sidewalk,

instead of a person who grew up less fortunate.

Special Thoughts

A Childs mind

A childs mind is a lot different from adults

It's fearful and also kind of fearless

Because we're not sure what is right

Which path leads to victory?

Or who to be friends with

We want our life to be successful

But we don't know if were doing things right

So we look up to our brothers, sisters, and parents

But remember we're small and your so big

So were kind of shy

So instead of coming out and saying what should I do?

We just admire our elders and watch there every move

Because the only thing going through our mind

Is I want to be like him

I want to be like her

She's successful and I'll be too

This is why some things go wrong

Jennifer Goldberg

Because the older people don't pay attention to this action

And they wind up making a mistake

So please make the right decisions

You know what they are deep down in your heart

But we don't know what it is yet

Because we haven't found our heart, we haven't

Searched deep down in our soul

So help these children,

at least until they have a mind of their own

Special Thoughts

<u>Please forgive me</u>

Something bad happened today and I just know its all my fault.

I made a mistake, a terrible sin, and I don't know what to do. everything I try just makes it worse. Now I'm starting to cry.

So please oh mighty trees, reach out to him and show him my sorrow and my gratitude.

Please nature talk to him and show him how I feel.

Oh please mighty god, lord of my creation,

forgive me now and let me know how to fix this horrifying sin.

I sit in the corner away from the world, trying to pretend that nothing ever happened.

I close my eyes and try to ignore it, but doing this just makes me feel worse. I'm sorry and regret everything that happened. There's nothing more I can do,

Jennifer Goldberg

but beg to you.

So please oh mighty trees, reach out to him and show him my sorrow and my gratitude.

Please nature talk to him and show how I feel.

Oh please mighty god lord of my creation,

forgive me now and let me know how to fix this horrifying sin.

Now I feel as if my heart will break in two, I can hardly think of anything to do.

I regret with my heart, I regret it with my soul, but there's nothing more to say, but please forgive me. I ran out of ideas, so I'll just say this and maybe you'll feel my true emotions.

So please oh mighty trees, reach out to him and show him my sorrow and my gratitude.

Please nature talk to him and show how I feel.

Special Thoughts

Oh please mighty god lord of my creation,

forgive me now and let know how to fix this horrifying sin.

There's nothing more to say, nothing more to beg of you. So may you have felt my heart and understand how I feel. Please, oh mighty lord of mine, tell me what to do. I can't take this any longer.

I feel I'm hated here.

So when you understand my solemn soul, speak to me, so I can forgive myself for this horrifying sin.

Printed in the United States
6236